Jimmy :D
Always love in freedom,
dream without limits,
never forget that you are loved
in all your worlds…

There once was a fish that swam in the vast ocean.
For it is the way of all fish.

The fish understood water and its rules, it knew
how to join the currents, and to swim in perfect
synchrony with his school of fish, creating patterns
of beauty and precision, never in disharmony with
his group.

The fish loved water, for this was its element, as it
should be in the life of every fish.

There was also a bird that flew free in the sky. For it is the way of all birds.

The bird understood air and its winds, the playful clouds, and the gentle breeze that lifted its flight, the freedom and solitude of heights.

The bird loved air, for this was its element, as it should be in the life of every bird.

In the ever-changing dance of life, some things meet, others never do. In this particular case, the fish saw the bird, the bird saw the fish…

The bird did not know the fish, nor did it understand the limits of the ocean where it swam…

The fish did not know the bird, nor did it understand the limitless sky where it flew…

Curiosity sparked in them, as they observed each other carefully… And the days went by, as it tends to be with time.

The bird would dive into the ocean, the fish would leap into the sky.

The fish would leap into the sky, the bird would dive into the ocean.

As is often common, when something is closely observed, understanding is born, shortly thereafter fascination follows, and little by little love arrives...

The bird discovered the limits of the ocean and its rules.

The fish discovered the limitless freedom of the sky and its winds.

As it is a natural occurrence between two beings that share love, both their worlds interweave. With each leap, drops of water sparkled in the air, with each dive, air bubbles danced in the water. Even though they were opposites, there were moments of harmony between them.

With love, new things are born, opposites unite, new possibilities arise…

From a fish of the ocean and a bird of the sky a new mixed being was born, it belonged both to the ocean and to the sky. A new spirit that understood both worlds; the ocean currents, and the blowing of winds.

The fish and the bird loved this being, for inside it lived the best of both of them.

*In the natural order of things, there are clear rules:
that which belongs to the ocean must swim back to it,
that which belongs to the sky must fly back to it.*

With every leap the fish felt
more and more separated
from its element, it missed
the deep currents, the exact
rules of its school of fish.

With every dive the bird
yearned for the limitless sky,
the breeze that lifted its flight,
the company of clouds.

As is natural in life, there must be conditions for things to work. In the particular case of love, there is only one: that which you love, you must set free...

The fish loved the bird and wished it happiness. The bird loved the fish and wished it happiness. Their worlds were so different that it would not allow for a long coexistence, it was time for each to return to its own universe.

The fish leapt into the sky for the last time, feeling the warm breeze, offering bright water droplets to its bird...

The bird dove into the vast ocean for the last time, feeling the soft movement of the water, offering colorful bubbles to its fish...

In that manner, with a light soul, each followed its own path with gratitude and joy, keeping a profound love for that mixed being, the best of them both.

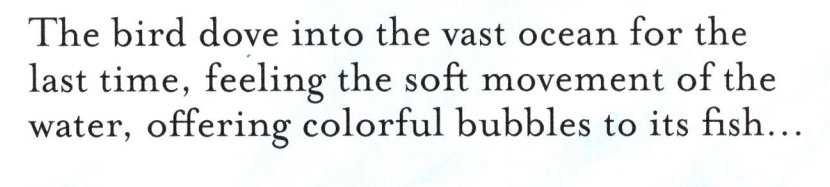

In life, each encounter is a gift… from the encounter of a fish of the ocean and a bird of the sky a mixed being remained, that through love, united two different worlds…

As time went by the bird joyfully flew between clouds with this mixed being, that understood the gentle breeze and the freedom of heights.

As time went by the fish swam joyfully in perfect synchrony with this mixed being, that understood the water currents and the rules of the ocean.

Forever united
 in this new being.
 The end

Neri García was born in Mexico City. She studied Graphic Design in the University of the Americas in Puebla, Mexico. She holds an MFA in Visual Communication from the Universität Gesamthochschule Kassel, Germany. She worked as a designer and art director in Mexico, Germany and the United States for different clients in a variety of industries.

Currently, she lives in Miami with her son Jimmy and her dog Glucklich. She is a Graphic Design professor at the University of Miami.

She continues to work as a freelancer in graphic design and illustration projects. In her free time, she writes and illustrates children's books. "Two Places to Love" is her first bilingual book.

Special thanks to: Olga Malykh , Paul Delbo, Natalia Obregón, Kathryn Van Cooper, Rick Navarro and Rene Alvarez for their help with the translation of this story.

www.ingramcontent.com/pod-product-compliance
Lightning Source LLC
Chambersburg PA
CBHW060839290526
45792CB00006BB/1983